Service-Oriented Architecture

FOR
DUMMIES

by Judith Hurwitz, Robin Bloor,
and Carol Baroudi

WILEY

Wiley Publishing, Inc.

Service-Oriented Architecture For Dummies®

Published by
Wiley Publishing, Inc.
111 River Street
Hoboken, NJ 07030-5774
www.wiley.com

WILEY

About the Authors

Judith Hurwitz was one of the first analysts to recognize the business value of emerging technologies. In 1992, she founded Hurwitz Group, an industry-leading software research and consulting organization. She is President of Hurwitz & Associates, a research and consulting firm focused on identifying customer benefit and best practices for buyers and sellers of information technology in the U.S. and Europe.

Robin Bloor is a partner in Hurwitz & Associates and founder and intellectual driving force behind the U.K. analysis company, Bloor Research, founded in 1989. He is an acknowledged expert in many areas of IT, including software development, IT security, systems management, operating systems, databases, and hardware architecture.

Carol Baroudi is a veteran *For Dummies* author and eager co-conspirator with Judith and Robin. Clocking more than 30 years in the computer industry, she has been writing *For Dummies* books since 1993. As an industry analyst, her primary technology focus is on emerging technologies, and SOA certainly fits the bill.

Dedications

Judith dedicates her part of the book to her family, Warren, Sara, David, and Elaine.

Robin dedicates his part of the book to Judy for her encouragement, support, and advice.

Carol dedicates her part of the book to Josh with all her love.

Authors' Acknowledgements

We thank our friends at IBM: Steve Mills, Robert Le Blanc, Sandy Carter, Glenn Hintz, and Martha Leversuch. Thanks also to Marcia Kaufman, Fern Halper, Fran Howarth, and Carol Caliendo, our cohorts at Hurwitz & Associates.

Publisher's Acknowledgments

We're proud of this book; please send us your comments through our online registration form located at www.dummies.com/register/.

Some of the people who helped bring this book to market include the following:

Acquisitions, Editorial, and Media Development

Project Editor: Paul Levesque

Acquisitions Editor: Katie Feltman

Copy Editor: Andy Hollandbeck

Technical Editor: Arnold Reinhold

Editorial Manager: Leah Cameron

Media Development Associate Producer: Richard Graves

Editorial Assistant: Amanda Foxworth

Sr. Editorial Assistant: Cherie Case

Composition Services

Project Coordinator: Kristie Rees

Layout and Graphics: Carl Byers, Denny Hager, Heather Ryan, Alicia B. South, Julie Trippetti

Proofreaders: Jessica Kramer

Publishing and Editorial for Technology Dummies

Richard Swadley, Vice President and Executive Group Publisher

Andy Cummings, Vice President and Publisher

Mary Bednarek, Executive Acquisitions Director

Mary C. Corder, Editorial Director

Publishing for Consumer Dummies

Diane Graves Steele, Vice President and Publisher

Joyce Pepple, Acquisitions Director

Composition Services

Gerry Fahey, Vice President of Production Services

Debbie Stailey, Director of Composition Services

Table of Contents

Introduction

● ●

*W*elcome to *Service-Oriented Architecture (SOA) For Dummies.* We're very excited by the topic and hope our enthusiasm is contagious. We believe SOA is the most important technology initiative facing businesses today. SOA is game-changing, and early SOA successes make it clear that SOA is here to stay. We hope this little book is enough to ground you in SOA basics as well as whet your appetite for even more SOA subjects.

Foolish Assumptions

Try as we might to be all things to all people, when it comes to writing a book, we had to pick who we thought would be most interested in *Service-Oriented Architectures For Dummies.* Here's who we think you are:

- ✔ **You're smart.** You're no dummy. Yet the topic of service-oriented architecture gives you an uneasy feeling; you can't quite get your head around it and, if pressed for a definition, might try to change the subject.

- ✔ **You're a businessperson who wants little or nothing to do with technology,** but you live in the 21st century and find you can't actually escape it. Everybody around is saying "SOA this" and "SOA that," so you think you'd better find out what they're talking about.

- ✔ **Alternatively, you're an IT person who knows a heck of a lot about technology,** but this SOA stuff is new and everybody says it's something different. Once and for all, you want the whole picture.

Whoever you are, welcome. We're here to help.

How This Book Is Organized

This little version of *Service-Oriented Architecture For Dummies* tries to fit a whole bunch of information into a few pages. We do have a giant version chock-full of even more information, but this mini version is meant to give you a good conceptual understanding of what SOA is and why we think it's important.

You'll notice that the first four chapters slowly but surely lead you down an (increasingly complex) path to SOA understanding. (We consider these chapters to be the meat of the book.) Chapter 5 (entitled "Real Life with SOA") pulls back to tell the story of Delaware Electric's own journey to SOA, and we close things off with a "SOA Quick Start" (Chapter 6), which is meant to do just that — give you pointers on how to get started with SOA.

Icons Used in This Book

 We think this is a particularly useful point to pay attention to.

 Pay attention. The bother you save may be your own.

 You might be sorry if this little tidbit slips your mind.

Where to Go from Here

We revisit many of the topics we introduce in this little book in the full-length edition of *Service-Oriented Architecture For Dummies*. There, we spend many pages describing things we barely had space to introduce here. Indeed, we have full chapters on the Enterprise Service Bus, the SOA registry, and XML, for example, and we introduce more SOA topics that didn't make it into this slimmed-down edition. If we have piqued your interest, we encourage you to try the full-fledged version of *Service-Oriented Architecture For Dummies*.

Chapter 1

SOA What?

· ·

· ·

*A*lthough service-oriented architecture (SOA) may very well be the hottest topic being bandied about by IT vendors across the globe today, no one (not even the IT vendors) can claim that SOA has established itself to such an extent that everybody just knows what everybody is talking about when they talk about SOA.

In fact, we're sure that the most common response to hearing this particular three-letter combination is still "What's SOA?" — which is why we wrote this book. We suspect, dear reader, that you've already googled or asked trusted friends the "What's SOA?" question, but the answers you've gotten so far have been, well, inadequate. The short answer is that SOA is a new approach to building IT systems that allows business to leverage existing assets and easily enable the inevitable changes required to support the business. (We get very specific in Chapter 2.) However, right now, we think the more important question is "Why should I care about SOA?" We're going to try to answer this question first — take a deep breath — by telling you exactly why you should care:

> The promise of service-oriented architecture is to liberate business from the constraints of technology.

From our perspective, one of the most important aspects of SOA is that it is a *business* approach and methodology as much as it is a *technological* approach and methodology. SOA enables business to make business decisions *supported* by technology instead of making business decisions *determined* by or *constrained* by technology.

We pronounce SOA to rhyme with boa. Stretching it out by clearly articulating each letter ("S-O-A") is perfectly acceptable, but may leave you stymied when we say things like "SOA What?"

Business Lib

One of the myths that plagues business today is that senior management is in charge. Yes, we know who holds the title, but a management title is a lot like the title to a car. The title is one thing, and the keys are another. And, though no one ever saw it coming, the keys to the business have been slipping, little by little, into the hands of IT. And this is not good for the business. What is not good for business is ultimately not good for IT because without the business, IT ceases to exist.

Now, we are not advocating that business should or can wrest the keys from the hands of IT. Our businesses are inextricably tied to technology. No sizable business can function without IT — it's as simple as that. However, we are advocating a New World Order — an order where business and IT not only work together to determine how the business should operate, but also work together to make it a reality using SOA. But before we go marching off to save the world, we have some more explaining to do. We think a story will help.

Once upon a Time: Illustrating the Need for SOA

Once upon a time, there was an insurance company called ABC Property and Casualty. When ABC was born, oh, maybe 150 years ago, it began by selling insurance policies to factories and manufacturers. In those days, there were no computers to mess things up. A nice person sent a letter inquiring about a policy. A smart person set a rate and hoped that nothing caught fire or blew up. ABC thrived for more than a hundred years. But then, things got complicated. Other companies started to steal their business. Customers were asking for insurance for different kinds of risk. ABC had to change or die.

In the 1980s, ABC bought computers and hired programmers and built software applications to support its business. Over time, it bought software packages from different suppliers to help it continue to compete. It bought or built business applications to solve problems all over the company — one at a time. For example, it bought an application for the corporate finance department, created one to handle customer claims, and procured other applications to manage research information about what type of accidents were most common under what circumstances.

This worked well for many years, until, in the late '80s and early '90s, ABC found itself competing against financial services companies who, out of the blue, decided *they* could sell insurance, too. Suddenly, ABC needed to find new ways to make money that didn't cost too much. Its leaders thought about exciting new solutions based on their knowledge of their business and their customers and through new, cool *technology*.

In addition, Management thought ABC could better compete by acquiring some other insurance companies with complementary products. ABC could sell these new products to existing ABC customers and sell ABC's products to the customers of the companies they acquired. These smart guys and gals understood business strategy. Everyone got really excited until . . .

Management talked to IT, and IT said, "This is really, really exciting, but we have a *small* problem."

"What could it be?" cried Management.

"It is this," said IT. "We can no longer simply buy or build more programs to implement our new moneymaking, cost-saving ideas. Everything we want to do has to work in concert with what we already have. The very running of our company depends on all of the business applications that we have built and acquired over years working together smoothly — the programs to tally the money coming in, the programs to administer the claims processing going out, to do risk analysis, premium billing, payroll, invoicing, and sales commission calculation. When you come right down to it, our company is the aggregation of all our programs. Everything we need in order to carry out our day-to-day business functions — all our policies and information, including all the information about our customers — is locked inside these programs."

"Well," said Management, "You can just write new programs to tie everything together. We'll *integrate* and we will all be very happy."

And IT said, "Yes, it is possible to *integrate*, but integrating will take *a very, very long time*. Integrating will take at least eighteen months, maybe two years, and by then you may want more changes that will take another eighteen months or two years and by then it may be too late. And," IT continued, "*It will cost lots and lots of money.*"

Management and IT were very sad. They knew that ABC would not survive if they couldn't find *a new way of thinking*. So they began asking everyone they knew if there was any way to save ABC. They searched and they studied and they prayed until one day a package arrived from Amazon.com. And in that package were several copies of a yellow and black book. And on the cover of the yellow and black books, they read *Service-Oriented Architecture For Dummies*.

Both Management and IT took copies of the book and read. They were very excited to discover that they didn't have to throw stuff away and that they could reap benefits in a short period of time. In the end, they came up with a *new* strategy, one based on four key elements:

1. The IT organization will partner with the line of business managers to create a high-level map of what the business will look like.

2. The IT organization will create a flexible structure that will turn key IT software assets into reusable services that can be used no matter how the business changes. These services will span everything from business processes and best practices, to consistent data definitions, to code that performs specific business functions.

3. The IT organization will only use accepted industry standards to link these software assets together.

4. The IT organization will use the service-oriented architecture concept described in the rest of this book to begin to create business services that are consistent with the way the business operates.

Together, Management and IT began a journey, and, as far as we know, they are living happily ever after . . . In Chapter 5, we give you a real-life case study from a real-life company you may know that indeed is alive and well and living happily on its *Journey to SOA*.

Saving Bundles by Using What You Have

One of the biggest deals, SOA-speaking, is the idea that you don't throw things out. You take the stuff (software assets and other ilk) that you use every day — well, the *best* of the stuff you use every day — and package it in a way that lets you use it, reuse it, and keep on reusing it.

One problem common to companies that have been around for a while is that they have lots of similar programs. Every time a department wants something slightly different, the department builds its own version of that something so that, across a particular company, you can find umpteen versions of more or less the same program — with, of course, slight variations. This happens a lot when one company acquires another and finds that they have similar (but not identical) programs purporting to do the same thing.

These slight variations are precisely what make systems very complicated and impossible to maintain — if you make a change in business policy that affects the sundry applications, for example, you have to find and change each and every instance in every application that is affected. And even the slightest difference in implementation can result in inconsistencies — not a nice thing to find when those compliance auditors come snooping.

With SOA, these important programs become *business services.* (We talk more about this later, so don't worry.) You end up with one single business service for a given function that gets used everywhere in your organization. With SOA, when you need to change a business policy, you change it in one place and, because the same service is used everywhere, you have consistency throughout your organization.

For example, you know that if you decide to create a new department in your organization, you are not going to create a new Accounting department, new Human Resources department, new Legal department, new Cleaning department, new Training department, and new Travel department to go along with it. We trust that you will use your existing Accounting department (you may have to add staff), your existing HR, and your existing Cleaning, Training, and Travel departments to — note the expression — *service* this new department.

The problem is that, over time, IT — not those nice folks in the IT department today, but IT *over time* — ends up embedding redundant function in individual programs everywhere in the organization. That redundancy, just like having separate Accounting, HR, Legal, Cleaning, Training, and Travel departments for every department, is what SOA will ultimately eliminate — giving you the same obvious benefits of scalability, consistency, and maintainability.

With SOA, business managers work with IT to identify business services. Together, they determine policy and best practices. These policies and best practices become *codified business services,* impervious to the whims and fancies of errant engineers, audacious autocrats, tyrannous technologists, business bigots, and other such unsavory suspects. No more random acts of software. No more self-designated despots. Hail the New World Order!

Expanding Your SOA to Customers, Partners, and Suppliers

If you dance any kind of formal dance, from the cha-cha to the waltz, you know that form matters. It is the *form* that allows you to dance with someone you've never met. When both partners truly know the form, they move in tandem, are flexible, and navigate with **ease and** grace.

SOA is form. It enables the business to move, change, partner, and reinvent itself with **ease and** grace. In the beginning, learning new steps requires focus and attention. Over time, SOA becomes second nature.

Implicit in the form are standards. Using industry-standard interfaces and creating business services without dependencies (more later, we promise) allows the business to change its business model, to re-orchestrate itself, and to partner dynamically.

You feel confident that the appliances that you plug in at home today will plug in equally well at the office or if you move across town. You may also be aware that if you travel abroad, you will likely need adapters. Clearly you can plug in anywhere that the standard interfaces agree, but where they are different, you must adapt. Likewise, although, in theory, you could create an infinite number of service-oriented architectures, working with industry standards set forth by standards bodies (later, later), enables autonomous entities (partners, customers, suppliers, hint, hint) to dance at the ball.

Focus on Function — Hide the Unsightly

In the next chapter, we talk a lot about architecture — but don't panic. We aren't going to go geeky on you. In fact, one big reason we think you're going to like SOA is that, with SOA, business gets to focus on business in a way that is supported rather than thwarted by technology. Like the plumbing in a well-designed home, SOA systems just works — the technical sophistcation is there, but it is almost invisible at the business layer. (We show and tell you all about this in the next chapter.) But right here in Chapter 1, we want you to consider what your life would be like if you could make your business act the way you want it to act without having to worry about technology.

SOA forces business managers and IT to talk in terms both sides understand. A business service is a business service is a business service. How that business service is implemented in the technology layer is the purview of IT, and business managers need not worry about it. Really. Trust us.

Why Is This Story Different from Every Other Story?

Perhaps you are skeptical. Perhaps, for as long as you can remember, IT has been promising yet another silver bullet to rid you of all business woes. We think now's a good time to repeat that SOA is not about "out with the old, in with the new." SOA is about *reuse*. SOA is about taking what you have and structuring it in a way that allows you not only to continue to use it, but to use it secure in the knowledge that future change will be simple, straightforward, safe, and fast. SOA is indeed a journey — it can't be built overnight. But organizations can begin SOA now and can benefit now. Ultimately, SOA renders a business more flexible — and IT more reliable, sustainable, extensible, manageable, and accountable.

We think SOA is the most important mandate facing business today. And because SOA is a joint venture between business managers and IT, we present the basics necessary for everyone to come to the table with a good grounding from a conceptual level. We won't give you a blow-by-blow technological diatribe — we promise.

Chapter 2

Noah's Architecture

- -

In This Chapter

▶ All about architectures

▶ Defining services and business services as part of a service-oriented architecture

▶ Defining service-oriented architecture

▶ Four complications

- -

*W*e're about to define service-oriented architecture. If you find our definition fraught with terms we haven't yet defined, you're right. Hold tight, well get there — we promise. Ready? Take a deep breath. . . .

We define a *service-oriented architecture* as a software architecture for building applications that implement business processes or services using a set of loosely coupled black-box components orchestrated to deliver a well-defined level of service.

Okay, now we're going to explain that definition.

What's an Architecture?

Before we go jumping off into explaining *service-oriented* architecture, we're going to start with just plain old architecture (from an information technology point of view) to make sure we're all on the same page.

In the beginning, there were programs, and programs were good, and programs needed no stinking architectures. And then there was business, and the business grew, and programs grew, and chaos was on the face of the business. And so, in an effort to create order, programmers adopted systematic structures to organize the programs and to help the business. And structures, be they strip malls or the Taj Mahal, or even Noah's Ark, are known as *architectures*. When we describe software structures, we call them, well, *software architectures*.

Every building has a structure of some sort. The idea of architecture implies thoughtful planning according to a set of guidelines or rules. (In a building, for example, the steelwork has to support both the current plans and future additions.) Some architectures are better than others. The same thing applies to software architectures. A good software architecture specifies how data is stored, how users interact, how programs communicate, and much, much more.

Business applications, the programs that make corporations run (from accounts receivable to order processing to warehouse management), need to access information from many different places. In the Good Old Days, a business unit would ask the IT department to create an application to solve a specific business problem. To accomplish this goal, the IT department would write a set of customized programs. These programs included all sorts of things related to the problem being solved, the data being used, and even the hardware the newly created programs would run on. New problems to solve meant new programs to write, and everyone lived happily ever after. Sort of.

Whatever structure the IT department created was the *architecture* of the systems they developed, and for the most part they were self-contained structures created to serve a particular function. They were not originally built to be connected to each other, and, like many an eclectic mix cobbled together over time, these disparate architectures make running the information technology of a contemporary company, well, uh, tough.

SOA to the rescue

Businesses keep changing and requests for new programs keep coming. What's new and different is the idea that businesses don't have to keep reinventing the wheel and that they can organize programs for easy reuse, for easy maintenance and support, for coherent, consistent results across their organizations, and for easily sharing their data and resources. And that, in a nutshell, is the idea behind a service-oriented architecture.

In a service-oriented architecture world, business applications are assembled using a set of building blocks known as *components* — some of which may be available "off the shelf," and some of which may have to be built from scratch. (We talk a lot more about components in Chapter 3, so if you feel compelled to learn more about components at this very instant, you can jump there. However, if you have a vague notion of what components probably are, we suggest you keep reading.)

The software architecture defines which software components to use and how these components interact with each other. Sounds pretty simple when we put it that way, but we're not going to hide the ugly truth from you: creating a service-oriented architecture takes thought, patience, planning, and time. We call it a journey, and depending on the size and scope of an organization, it may be a journey of years or even a decade. But you can start seeing returns on your SOA investment very quickly.

Basic architecture

We're going to start with a very simple example of a software architecture. (Don't worry. You'll get a look at more complex structures before the chapter's through.)

Figure 2-1 shows a simple example of a software architecture for an order-processing application that allows customers to place orders through the Internet. It has the following five components:

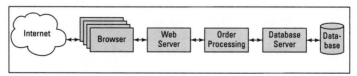

Figure 2-1: A simple software architecture.

✔ **The Browser** is located on a user's device that accesses the business application through a Web site. Many users can access the application at the same time, so many browsers may link to the Web server. The primary job of the browser is to display information and accept input from the user.

✔ **The Web Server** manages how the many Web pages are sent to the browsers of the users who are accessing the business application.

✔ **The Order Processing** application carries out the business process that is being executed. This component includes the company's best business practices.

✔ **The Database Server** reads data from a database and sends the data where it is needed.

✔ **The Database** is where data and the definitions of the business data are stored.

Information passes from the browser to the Web server to the order-processing application, which decides what to do next. The order processing application might pass data to the database server to write to disk, or it may request data from the database, or it may simply send information back to the browser through the Web server. What the order-processing application does depends upon the information and commands passed to it by the user.

Basic service

We all know what a service is — we pay for services all the time. We pay for electrical service, telephone service, and service at a restaurant. Using the restaurant example, we sit down at a table, consult a menu, give our order to the waiter, and the meal is delivered as soon as it is prepared. We pass a simple set of information to the waiter (what we want to eat and drink), and somehow, magically, the restaurant provides it. Usually, we do not see the food cooked or participate in its preparation or serving. That is the service that we pay for.

We can talk about the restaurant in terms of *components* and how they interact. (We say more about components in Chapter 3.) We order food from the server. The server sends or takes the order to the kitchen. The kitchen prepares the food and alerts the waiter, who then, we hope, brings us what we asked for. We are a component, the waiter is a component, and the kitchen is a component. The service-oriented architecture of the restaurant comprises these components and more — a cleaning component and a supply-ordering component, for example.

Business services

We can also talk about the restaurant in terms of *services*. In the complicated, convoluted, controversial contrivance called a corporation, services abound. It is no mean feat to discover and identify them all, but ultimately a business needs to. For now, we are going to introduce a formal definition of a business service.

We define a *business service* as *the logical encapsulation of business function.* In simple terms, we mean that you wrap up everything you have to do to make a particular business function happen and give that rolled-up something the name *business service.*

So, in our restaurant example, everything the kitchen has to do to prepare the meal, from chopping vegetables to cooking to plating could be called the "meal-preparation service." Everything the server does to extract the order from us (elucidate menu items, tell us what isn't available right now, suggest appetizers and side dishes, write down our order) could be rolled up into the "order-taking service."

Elementary service-oriented architecture

In a *service*-oriented architecture, business services interact with each other in ways similar to how the various services of the restaurant interact.

Now, you can think of the restaurant from two levels — from the business services level, which describes the functions and how they interact, and from an "implementation" point of view, that is, how the food actually gets prepared, how it actually gets onto the plate, and so forth. The various services pass information, ask for tasks to be performed, and serve up the results. We can illustrate this division of function by adding a new credit-checking component to our previous architecture diagram.

In Figure 2-2, we add a Credit Checking component. Its service is called on when new customers place an order to determine whether they are credit worthy. In the figure, we do not show or even care about how the credit checking is done. For the sake of simplicity, say that the credit checking software component is run by an external company and simply provides a service. The company using this credit checking software is confident that the service conducts a credit check in the right way.

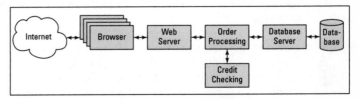

Figure 2-2: Adding a service-oriented component.

The Order Processing application simply requests the credit checking service and passes along the necessary information (a person's name and Social Security number). The Credit Checking component consults its information sources, does some calculations, and passes back a Credit Rating. The Credit Checking component may connect to many computers and consult many different data sources to calculate the credit rating by using a very sophisticated algorithm, but this is of no concern to the Order Processing application. As far as the Order Processing application is concerned, Credit Checking is just a *black box*.

Also, we need to emphasize that the Credit Checking component *does only Credit Checking*. It doesn't offer a wide range of services. It is precisely because the components have a narrowly defined scope — that is, they do "one thing" — that they can be used and reused as building blocks.

SOA's use and reuse of components makes it easier to build new applications as well as change existing applications. Using well-proven, tested components makes testing new applications easier.

It's So Simple; It Has Taken Only 40 Years . . .

You may be thinking, "Well, of course software should work this way. Isn't it always built to work this way?" The answer is no. It may surprise you, but the software industry has spent more than 40 years trying to get to the point where it can build *modular* software applications.

In the following sections, we explain why life in the world of corporate IT hasn't always worked the way we want it to work. We introduce four major complications and do our best to not only elucidate the complications but show you how service-oriented architecture resolves these complications.

Complication #1: Business logic and plumbing

To build a software application, you have to tell the computer how to do what you want, both in human terms — which we call *the business logic* — and in computer terms — the stuff we call *the plumbing*. (We will try to avoid getting scatological.)

Business applications are composed of lines of instructions (program code) that tell computers what actions to take. Some of these instructions are written as business logic ("add an item line to the order," for example), and some are simply plumbing (computer-level directives such as "check that the printer is available"). Both are necessary. If you do not describe the application's activity in simple business logic (purchase orders, products, customers, accounts, and so on), you quickly lose sight of what you are trying to achieve. If you do not describe in computer terms exactly how the computer should carry out its task, the software simply won't work.

Which brings us to one of the biggest problems in programming today: Because you need to control business logic and the plumbing at the same time, you need to set up your business logic and your plumbing as separate (if parallel) tracks. That involves a fair amount of work — as well as applying a particular lens to what is being developed — but it has to be done if you want to take full advantage of SOA.

For example, if you want to change the order in which particular business functions happen and you've kept your business logic separate from your plumbing, making these changes is no big deal using SOA. But if your business logic and your plumbing are one giant application, changes are costly and complicated and take time, require extensive testing, and are a very big deal indeed.

Many software components deal only with managing a specific aspect of computer plumbing. For example, Web servers manage the presentation of information to Web browsers, and database software manages how information is stored and retrieved. These components involve no business logic. Business logic needs to be as free of plumbing dependencies as possible.

With this in mind, we can now redraw our architecture diagram to be both a little bit more service-oriented *and* a little bit more general.

In Figure 2-3, we introduce the idea of a business layer and a plumbing layer, and in doing so, we introduce the idea of specific services. (For simplicity's sake we've left out the Web server and the browser). It works like this:

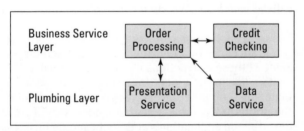

Figure 2-3: A service-oriented view.

- ✔ **The Business Service Layer** consists of software components that provide and carry out specific business functions. Another way to say this is that they *deliver specific business services.*

- ✔ **The Plumbing Layer** consists of components that provide all those services involving actual computer resources to components in the Business Service Layer. Here are two such components:

- *Presentation Service:* The Web server called by a different name

- *Data Service:* The database server called by a different name

By splitting the architecture diagram into two layers, we divide the software that is of direct relevance to the business — because it carries out business functions — from the software that supports the use and management of computer resources. With our SOA-based approach, we have, to some degree, divided business logic from plumbing.

Don't panic. Remember that we mentioned in the beginning of the chapter that SOA is a *journey.* Now's a good time to take another deep breath.

"All is well and good," you're saying, "in a hypothetical world. But we have real systems that have been in place for years, and in some cases decades. We can't exactly throw everything out and start from scratch." We know. We have a solution. Trust us.

Complication #2: The not-so-green field

Complication #2 is that businesses don't live in a perfect world. They cannot start from scratch, which means they're dependent on legacy systems that are in place and operational right now — and, besides, they certainly don't have the time or budget to start from scratch. The good news is that SOA is a journey (remember that part?), that it takes place over time, and best of all, *it reuses what already exists.* SOA is not "out with the old, in with the new"; it is about separating the wheat from the chaff so that you can have your cake and eat it, too. (We like mixing metaphors.)

With SOA, you can make use all your existing business applications. True, you may need to change them a little in order to include them in a SOA, but it is possible and it is not all that hard. For example, you can treat an entire application as a service, or you can take some code out of an application and make just that code into a service.

In Figure 2-4, you'll notice that we've added an existing application. Now, our Internet order-processing system uses both a Credit Checking component and an Invoicing component. It interacts with the existing Invoicing system to send out an invoice. To make it possible for the Invoicing system to work in this way, we create a simple "adapter."

Now, the "simple adapter" may not be so simple for business folks to create, but the idea is simple enough to understand. SOA uses very specific, industry-agreed-upon standards to create interfaces which make it possible for various components of the SOA to talk to each other. In the full-length edition of *Service-Oriented Architecture For Dummies* we get very explicit about these adapters and how they manage to talk to each other. For now, leave the creating to us and assume that when the time comes, you (or someone near and dear to you) will be able to create all the adapters you need.

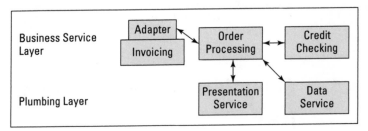

Figure 2-4: SOA with an existing application.

After you have all the required elements of a SOA in place, you can include an existing application or piece of an application within the SOA framework. Sounds great, but before you go out and start plugging everything lying about the office into your planned SOA — coffee machine included — you should know that we still have quite a few SOA components to discuss. Before we can do that, however, we still need to talk about Complications #3 and #4.

Complication #3: Application archaeology

Despite doing your best to split the architecture between a business layer and the plumbing layer, you'll likely find that almost all of the business layer components will still include some "plumbing" activities. This is because many of the business layer components come from existing applications, and existing business applications were likely built in very different ways, at different times, by different people, and for different reasons, maybe even using different computers.

Unlike a PC that you might hold onto for three or four years, application software tends to hang around a company for decades. Therefore, one company could have hundreds of applications that are all designed in different ways. Programs that are still in use from prior eras of technology are fondly referred to as *legacy code* and include mainframe applications, client/server applications, and just about everything that is functional that existed before you started your job.

These applications contain a lot of company knowledge. Many of these systems are the foundation for how business is done. They are used to bill customers and transfer funds. Even if you consider these applications to be ugly, they perform essential work.

Digging in the dirt

Consider the layers of applications on which your current business runs as archaeological layers. If you had to understand in detail how each layer works, how each is connected to various components, and how the thing is managed, it would take years and, because business and its applications are continually changing, you would never be done. Fortunately, you don't have to scrounge around playing archaeologist. You can wallow in blissful ignorance and simply ignore layers of code. Just as builders hide wiring and plumbing behind the walls — out of sight except where absolutely necessary — engineers hide a lot of complicated, messy code in convenient "black boxes."

The magical black box

We use the term *black box* in the traditional sense to mean a component or device whose workings are not understood or accessible by the user. Many programmers, for example, do not know how a CPU works but understand how to use it to execute programs. Similarly, a user may not know how a spreadsheet is designed but understands how to use it to create a sales forecast.

Intelligent black-boxing is an important aspect of SOA. With a SOA, you can build a whole new computing environment using all of the resources that you already have by treating many components as black boxes. Particularly, you need to treat existing application components as black boxes, making them accessible by adding adapters. For example, use a black box to include older plumbing services that still work. The black box avoids your spending money to replace something that works just fine. Or, as the sages say, "If it ain't broke, don't fix it."

Complication #4: Who's in charge?

So far so good. You are wrapping your ugly code into nice black boxes, making services out of existing applications, and life is wonderful. Right? Uh, not exactly. How exactly are components strung together to ensure the end-to-end service you expect? For example, how do you know that, when you place your restaurant order, food (specifically the food you ordered) will be prepared and delivered to you in a timely fashion?

Since any SOA you can think of is orders of magnitude more complex than our restaurant example — many more components, for starters — it behooves you to ask, "Who's running the show?" You have every good reason to be concerned about this because you don't want to have to worry about whether all the components have compatible plumbing. If the plumbing for one component doesn't work with the plumbing for several other components, how will an end-to-end process work? If it fails, how will you know?

Stymied? As an example of black-boxing a problem — that is, wrapping it up so you don't have to contend with intricacies that don't interest you — we're now going to let you know that any and all problems associated with the end-to-end processing of components are dealt with by a little something called the _SOA Supervisor._ So, no need to worry, because the SOA Supervisor will take care of things. The SOA Supervisor acts something like a traffic cop and helps prevent SOA accidents.

If you want to know exactly how the SOA Supervisor gets the job done, we refer you to the full-length edition of _Service-Oriented Architecture For Dummies._

Figure 2-5 adds our own little graphical depiction of the SOA Supervisor to our overall SOA model. Notice that we have also made the computer network and the Internet visible, for two reasons:

✔ Doing so more accurately depicts how software components actually connect with each other across a computer network. In most cases, applications run on separate server machines that connect via the network or possibly over the Internet.

✔ The SOA Supervisor needs to connect to every other component within the SOA in order to do its job. (If we drew each of the connections in, the diagram would get very busy very quickly.)

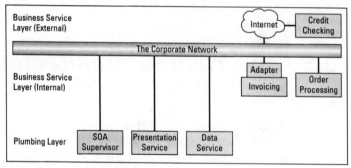

Figure 2-5: The SOA Supervisor.

Taking a look at Figure 2-5, you can see that the SOA Supervisor manages the end-to-end computer process created by connecting all the other software components together. In our depiction, applications are divided between *external* components (components outside the corporate network) and *internal* components (components inside the corporate network). (The Credit Checking component, for example, is an external component that is connected through the Internet.)

One of the SOA Supervisor's responsibilities is to monitor the various components within the SOA. The SOA Supervisor directly monitors only things in its purview. However it can also monitor results and responses from services provided from the outside.

You certainly will not be able to do much if an external service suddenly fails or goes very slowly. However, with internal components, the SOA Supervisor not only monitors the whole service that a component provides but may initiate corrective activity if things start to go wrong.

Now, with regard to the corporate computer network depicted in Figure 2-5, we do have to admit that an actual network can be a complex arrangement of networking hardware (switches, routers, hubs, and so forth) and connections (copper wires, fiber optic wires, and wireless connections), with computers of various kinds attached at various points. However, in line with our black-box approach to hiding complexity, you can think of the corporate computer network as a kind of pipe. The thing to be concerned about, more than anything else, is whether the pipe can accommodate the flow of data that is required.

Service-Oriented Architecture — Reprise

It has taken us a mere 14 pages to expand on our definition of a service-oriented architecture. Just to refresh your memory, a service oriented architecture is *an architecture for building business applications as a set of loosely coupled black-box components orchestrated to deliver a well-defined level of service by linking together business processes.*

Admittedly, this definition doesn't yet flow trippingly from the tongue. However, a sustainable, reusable, extensible approach to business and technology that is already providing huge competitive advantage to organizations around the globe *does* flow from it. Here's a little elucidation:

- ✔ **SOA is for building business applications.** Many legitimate approaches to software architecture exist, and SOA is not intended for building every kind of software. It is intended explicitly for building *business* applications.

- ✔ **SOA is a *black-box component architecture*.** SOA deliberately hides complexity wherever possible, and the idea of the black box is integral to SOA. The black box enables the reuse of existing business applications by adding a fairly simple adapter to them, no matter how they were built.

✔ **SOA components are *loosely coupled*.** The term "loosely coupled" refers to how two components interact with a SOA. One component passes data to another component and makes a request. The second component carries out the request and, if necessary, passes data back to the first. The emphasis is on simplicity and autonomy. Each component offers a small range of simple services to other components.

A set of loosely coupled components does the same work that used to be done inside tightly structured applications, but the components can be combined and recombined in myriad ways, making the overall IT much more flexible. We talk a lot more about loose coupling in *Service-Oriented Architecture For Dummies* — the chunky edition.

✔ **SOA components are orchestrated to link together through business processes to deliver a well-defined level of service.** SOA creates a simple arrangement of components that can, collectively, deliver a very complex business service. Simultaneously, SOA must provide acceptable service levels. To that end, the architecture embodies components that ensure a dependable service level. Service level is directly tied into the best practices of conducting business — commonly referred to as *business process management*. We have a lot more to say about business process management, but not until Chapter 4.

Why SOA? Better Business and Better IT

SOA can make it easier and faster to build and deploy IT systems that directly serve the goals of a business. Contemporary business is completely reliant on its IT, and never have business and IT needed to be more aligned. The very survival of a business hinges on its ability to adapt its IT to meet ever-changing business challenges. SOA integrates business and IT into a framework that simultaneously leverages existing systems and enables business change. A SOA enables the business to keep its focus on business and allows IT to evolve and keep pace in a dynamically changing world.

We divide the world of SOA into the business service layer and the plumbing layer, where the business service layer contains your business logic and your plumbing contends with your computing resources. Business managers need not understand the intricacies of the plumbing layer and everything it contains. If you mentally subtract out the plumbing layer, you are left with a view of your software that shows all the business services that applications provide, both inside your organization and to others that interact (technologically speaking) from outside, like your customers, business partners and suppliers. Looking at your organization's software resources in this way, you may be able to think about ways to improve or better exploit the software assets you have.

Likewise, if you mentally subtract out all the business functionality in your SOA vision, you are left with a set of plumbing services that your IT department is responsible for providing. We know that many of the "legacy" applications that run also have a good deal of plumbing in them, and the plumbing layer does not replace that. However, SOA enables an IT department to choose how it will evolve toward providing a "service-oriented architecture" and in time may obviate a good deal of lousy plumbing.

SOA doesn't guarantee a happier, healthier life, free from business concerns. However, movement toward SOA is usually a movement toward freedom and flexibility and bodes well for the longevity of an organization and for the sanity of those usually held responsible.

Chapter 3

Not So Simple SOA

"*O*K, if SOA's so wonderful, what's the catch?" you shrewdly ask. Like a lot of things worth having, SOA takes work and time — *and* it's really worth it. SOA represents a new world order in which business leadership and technology leadership together navigate the business challenges of the "All Technology, All The Time" era we inhabit.

If you want to be a part of this new world order, you have to have some fluency in the basic concepts. That's why we're here — to help you with those basic concepts. If you can remember back 10 or 15 years, you might not have known what e-mail was, and you had never surfed the Web — we know, some of us were writing *The Internet For Dummies* back then. For businesses everywhere, the concepts we're introducing now are every bit as revolutionary and important as the Internet was 10 years ago, and we have confidence that when you're through with us (or vice versa), you'll be no dummy.

Components and Component Wannabes

Traditional software applications are not very flexible. It is the sad truth. To be flexible — meaning, to move and bend (change) and not break — requires malice aforethought. Well, at least forethought. Flexible software is built from reusable pieces of software code known as *components*. When put together, components form an application, and when you write them well, the code can be used over and over again.

The difference between inflexible code and flexible code is a lot like the difference between a boombox and a *component* stereo system. In a fancy boombox, you might find a tape deck or two, a CD changer, an AM/FM radio, an amplifier, and speakers. When you go to the beach, it's all or nothing — you take the whole boombox, not just the CD player. With your extensible, flexible component stereo system, you can swap out your old tape deck or other components and plug in new ones whenever you want.

If you've had your boombox for five years, you know it's obsolete. It may play your CDs and your cassette tapes, but it certainly won't play your MP3 files. If you want to play your MP3 files on your boombox, you have to get radical and buy another boombox. (And just try to find one that plays your MP3 files and still plays your old cassettes!) And Heaven help you if you're stuck in pre-boombox land with one of those all-in-one systems that includes a turntable — because you can't imagine ever ditching your vinyl collection — but still want to play the newest tunes downloaded from an online music service.

Talk about wanting it all. It's tough enough trying to manage one's music collection, but just imagine the different kinds of systems at play in a corporate environment. In that world, you could think of your LPs and cassettes as legacy code, and, if they are important enough to you, you have to maintain the systems that support them. Such is the state of most corporate IT, but more about that later. Meanwhile, back to components. . . .

In software, as in stereo systems, the component model yields flexibility and reuse. And those great software architects on high have been talking about component architectures for more than a decade and have been expanding the concepts of reuse for more than half a century. (Subroutines, structured programs, data that is stored in centralized databases and object-orientation are all milestones in the advance of reusability.)

Making sure your components play nicely together

If one person sets about making components for his or her own personal use, he or she will undoubtedly get better at it over time and will eventually find precisely those components that help make the creation of new and different programs faster and easier — for himself or herself. However, as soon as that individual has to make things usable by other people or has to use other people's components, the need for agreement on how components should talk to each other takes center stage. Beyond that, the effort involved in letting other people know that you have great components, finding useful components other people have already built so you don't have to make them yourself, making sure everything really works as advertised, and all that niggling little stuff is enough to drive sane people away.

Fortunately for you, all this really is in the realm of IT, and many hard-working folks have been solving these problems so that you don't have to. The important point for you to remember is that not all components are reusable components. For components to be reusable, they *must* be constructed with standard interfaces — they must be created to talk to other components according to established and agreed-upon rules for talking to other components.

Of course, all this makes sense to most thinking individuals these days, but before the Internet became a significant influence in the software industry, software vendors did not necessarily want their components talking to other people's components. Competitive business practice encouraged the development of "proprietary" systems — systems that didn't talk to other people's systems — all in the name of making sure that customers didn't get it into their heads to "mix and match" software from different companies.

With the Internet, however, users everywhere were suddenly using common software — namely, the browser. Although Web surfers still use various browsers today, all browsers do pretty much the same thing — they help navigate to different sites, they display the contents of the Web pages, and then they allow interaction with the site. This is possible only because industrious, indefatigable, far-sighted individuals worked to create *standard* ways to tag information for display and *standard* ways to display tagged information. This standard is known as HTML (*H*yper*T*ext *M*arkup *L*anguage). You don't need to know more about HTML, but the concept of a standard interface is critical to your understanding of service-oriented architecture. For example, the browser interface has become the de facto standard user interface to all software. Even software that doesn't use the Web is now being designed with the assumption that you know how to point and click, you know what a link is and how to "navigate," even if where you're navigating to is another part of the software application.

Building in reusability

Building reusable components means creating a specific function or set of functions and supplying the standard interfaces that allow them to be used over and over again by generations yet unknown. To show you what we mean, we're going to extend our order-processing example from Chapter 2.

Our pumped-up example (see Figure 3-1) shows the order-processing application as comprising three sets of functions:

- ✔ The **Orders functions** let you add new orders, alter orders, delete orders, and inquire about orders.

- ✔ The **Customers functions** let you add new customers, change customer details, delete customers, and make inquiries about customers.

- ✔ The **Payments functions** let you accept payments by credit card or by customer account and to inquire about payments or accounts.

Order Processing		
Orders: New Order Alter an Order Delete an Order Order Inquiry	Customers: New Customer Alter Customer Delete Customer Customer Inquiry	Payments: Credit Card Customer Account Payment Inquiry Account Inquiry

Figure 3-1: Order processing as a set of functions.

All business applications have the same basic structure when looked at from the user perspective. They are made up of a set of functions that the user actually uses. Real-world order-processing applications might be a little more sophisticated than our example, including stuff like discount routines (that follow specific rules) or a rewards scheme (like air miles). No matter how complicated the application is, it always consists of a set of functions.

If you put this order-processing application on the Internet, customers could use their browsers as the standard user interface to place an order and enter personal (name and shipping location, for example) and payment information.

Of course, this "putting" of the order processing application on the Web requires the use of standard Web services interfaces. Once that's done, browsers can talk to it and it can live happily ever after. We are about to tell you all about Web services, so hang tight.

Web Services: The Early Days

In 1993, the first year *The Internet For Dummies* appeared in print, there were 130 Web sites and no browsers as we know them. (Our technical editor reminds us that by standing on your head and whispering secret incantations, you could telnet to a computer that had a browser on it.) The World Wide Web was covered in just one chapter in that first edition. We called early Web sites *brochureware* because the first attempts to use the Web for business often consisted of companies taking what they normally put into printed brochures and putting it up on the Web for the world to see. The sites were not interactive — they were just there.

It didn't take long (relatively speaking) for clever programmers to start offering services from the Web — Amazon.com, eBay, and Travelocity were among the first companies to demonstrate that the world was changing and that no one could ignore the Internet. The Web became a ubiquitous vehicle for the delivery of services — weather, news, real estate listings, tax forms, movie listings, distance learning, maps, directions. You name it; it's available on the Web.

At the same time, smart companies used the same technologies that delivered services to ordinary people to deliver services to other businesses or to other software applications. For example, IBM used a site that provided foreign currency exchange rates to help process staff expense reports. If the expense report included expenses submitted in a foreign currency, the program that captured the expenses went to the Web to get the appropriate foreign exchange rate for the same date as the expense item.

Strangely enough, the technologies that performed these services on the Web became known as *Web services*. We define a Web service as any piece of software that uses standard Web interfaces to communicate with other software containing Web service interfaces. (We could get a lot more technical, but we think that's enough right now.) The big point here is that Web services use *standard interfaces;* in fact, it is precisely *because* the interfaces are standard that Web services can

- Talk to each other in the first place.
- Provide a framework where different people from all over the globe can write new Web services that could potentially talk to Web services written by strangers. They use a common interface. Just like a plug and a socket, if the interfaces are standard, things just work.

Web services are fundamentally more useful than plain old application functions because all sorts of other programs can use them over and over again. This is possible because Web service interfaces use standards that have been agreed upon across the industry. Because everyone uses the standardized interfaces, like a socket and a plug, they just work. (Yes, we are repeating ourselves — but it's really, really important.)

If every function of the order-processing application is a Web service, other programs can use those functions and not have to reinvent the wheel. Figure 3-2 gives you an idea of what we mean. Here you can see the various order-processing applications broken down into reusable Web services. Using the very same Web service for the same function in every application that needs that function ensures that you get the same results everywhere the service is used. This can radically reduce errors, make change easier, and make the folks responsible for regulatory compliance a lot happier. Web services are good.

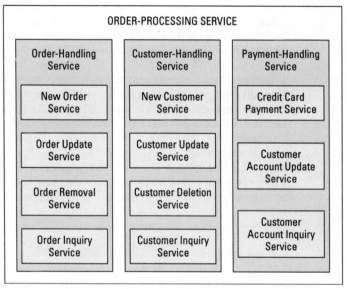

Figure 3-2: Breaking applications into Web services.

When Web Services Grow Up

Much to our frustration, a lot of folks think a service-oriented architecture is "Web services on steroids." Though critical to a service-oriented architecture, Web services are not the same thing as a service-oriented architecture, and here's why:

In order for business to free itself from technology, the business logic must be separated from the computer-level plumbing, as we describe in Chapter 2. Web services are in fact part of the plumbing. The business logic sits above the plumbing in the business services layer. Business logic constitutes *business services* that bring to the business the same efficiencies of reuse, ease of change, and consistency of results as Web services do on the programming level. And this is a big deal. Suddenly, business can reconfigure itself on the business services layer, and the appropriate technologies come along. Business can change without rewriting the world because business components, like stereo components, can be swapped in and out as needed.

The creation of a service-oriented architecture involves identifying the key *business services* and working top-down, versus bottom-up. Figure 3-3 shows order processing and credit checking as business services.

Identifying key business services is a major, major deal. Key business services are different for different companies. Making key business services into black boxes (as we talk about in Chapter 2) means that business can reorganize itself as needed. Services critical to the business become codified best practices, ensuring that business is being conducted under the explicit policies and principles defined by the business, rather than by the ad hoc practices that typically emerge and vary from one part of a company to another.

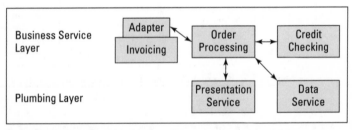

Figure 3-3: Top-down services in a SOA.

Defining Business Processes

Imagine for a moment that you have identified and created several key business services. You have converted all your business applications into a set of modular components with supporting Web service interfaces. Now that you have them, what do you want to do with them? Well, you probably want to string them together in ways that are useful to you. One way to string business services together is to create a business process.

We define a *business process* as *the codification of rules and best practices that constitute the business.* Simply stated, a business process is what has to happen for anything to get done. From a SOA perspective, a business process includes people, business services (which in turn comprise software applications that are collections of business functions), adapters (when needed to convert business functions into Web services), and some sort of process management activity that manages the flow of work between all the parts we just listed.

Business processes vary from business to business. In an insurance company, "claims handling" is a business process. In a hospital, "admitting a patient" is a business process. In a furniture store, "selling a cabinet" is a business process. Note that a business process is *not* by definition automated. It may indeed require manual participation or intervention. Great gains in efficiency come when a process is automated "from end to end."

The handy example

Figure 3-4 depicts a business process that embraces all of the end-to-end activities that occur from the time a customer places an order to when goods are dispatched to the customer. Here's a summary of what actually happens:

1. A clerk takes an order, perhaps checking on stock before accepting it. This process automatically links to another process, which checks to see if any stock reordering is necessary and places orders for new stock.

2. The order itself is passed to an assembler who gets every item on the order from a warehouse.

3. The assembler packages these items and sends them to dispatch.

4. Dispatch prints a delivery note that lists all the items assembled.

5. The order is packaged and shipped.

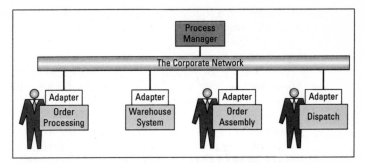

Figure 3-4: A business process.

The process management activity here involves linking together every manual activity and business function and passing data and instructions to the person or the business function when necessary. You can think of the people represented in the diagram as carrying out business functions that have not yet been automated or that cannot be automated (packing boxes, making phone calls, or any place where human involvement is required).

Business processes are production lines

Business processes typically have other business processes nested inside them like Russian dolls. "Taking and fulfilling an order" is a broad business process that consists of a collection of narrower business processes, such as recording the order, assembling the order, and dispatching the order. And exactly what is done and how it is done, for each such process, may vary.

If we model such *sub-processes* from a SOA perspective, the models consist of manual activities linked to application functions or to other manual activities, and the process management component takes care of the flow of activity from one activity to the next.

The flow of activity in business processes, as they are currently implemented by most organizations, is rarely fully automated and is often completely manual. Because process management is relatively new, many applications running in quite a number of organizations lack process management.

You can think of a business process as a production line. (If the flow of activity is automated, it really is a production line. The process follows a set path or, more likely, one of several possible paths, until it completes. The path the process follows is determined by the process management element. In following the path, various business functions are executed, and various manual tasks are carried out. The process can be repeated indefinitely.

New Applications from Old — Composite Applications

Another way to put your newly harvested Web services to use is to create new applications from them. *Composite applications* are applications built from the business functions of existing applications, with perhaps one or two new components added. Alternatively, you can think of them as business processes that have no manual elements.

Figure 3-5 shows a composite application. In this example, a business sets up a call center to sell directly to customers over the phone. It uses new SOA-enabled call center software to manage the flow of calls. This application consists of six business functions (C1, C2, . . .). The Call Center must be able to enter orders and process payments, so it requires all of the order-processing functions (O1, O2, . . .). The telephone sales staff needs to be able to check on stock, so they need, for example, function W4 from the warehouse system. Hiring the telephone sales staff requires all the functions (H1, H2, . . .) of the human resources and payroll systems. The call history module logs all the calls to the Call Center. Paying the sales staff a specially calculated commission may require writing a function (or module). A function to link call records to customer records must also be written.

Thread all of these things together and add the process manager component and, presto, you have a composite application that takes care of the call center operation. The composite application is built by the SOA, which sews all the components together.

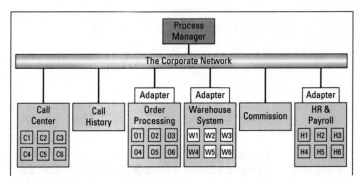

Figure 3-5: A composite application.

Toward end-to-end process

When you start thinking in terms of end-to-end processes, you have to sacrifice a view of the world that is fundamentally based on application silos. If you've ever crossed grain-growing fields, you probably remember the tall, autonomous structures that store grain. These structures are independent and free standing — and, most importantly, are not designed to have any connection with silos found anywhere else. In contemporary business IT parlance, *siloed applications* are those applications built specifically for immediate and exclusive use by one specific set of users with no intention or preparation for their use by others. Application silos, often harboring mission-critical code, blight the landscape of most organizations.

Siloed applications were built to satisfy the needs of one specific department or section of a company. It happened partly because of the way companies were organized and partly because of the way applications were built. Each department did what it could to ensure that it had the applications that served its specific needs.

The inability to easily integrate the pieces was no secret. Everyone knew there was an integration problem. To some extent, Enterprise Resource Planning (ERP) software vendors such as SAP and Oracle addressed this problem by pre-integrating a set of the most commonly used components, such as human resources (HR) and financial accounting. But such solutions went only so far and were of no help in specialized areas or when anomalies emerged.

Siloed applications generate the following two (very specific) problems:

> ✔ **Inconsistent data definitions:** Simply stated, applications built at different times or by different people often define the same set of data differently.
>
> ✔ **Duplication of software process:** Companies often have many applications that require the same program function in many different applications. Similar to inconsistent data definitions, duplicated software processes result in wasted time and effort.

The problems of siloed applications are frequently masked by flexible staff who compensate for computer systems that don't work well. While the immediate problem appears to be solved, the consequences of this ad hoc approach may prove dire. In a world that is demanding accountability in the form of regulatory compliance and audit, these behaviors are certainly suspect. SOA is very good for cleaning up these kinds of discrepancies — with SOA, the exact same function is performed the exact same way every time.

Adopting business processes and composite applications

SOA is conceptually different from traditional software architectures and requires you to think in new ways. We suggest you start tearing down your application silos and replacing them with end-to-end business processes and composite applications. Why? Because application silos are brittle, hostile to change, difficult to maintain, and make for unsupportable, inefficient, intransigent IT. Business processes and composite applications render the organizations they support more supple, extensible, and responsive to change.

As you well know, you can't change everything at once. One nice thing about SOA is that you can change things gradually, over time, knowing all the while that the changes you are making make future changes easier. Previous IT investments usually "ripped and replaced" still earlier investments with brand new somethings. With SOA, you don't rip down a silo and start from scratch. As you gently dismantle it, you salvage what's good and form it into reusable components. SOA allows you to harvest those early investments and plant them in renewable, reusable, fertile soil. Gosh, we're getting downright agrarian.

Chapter 4

SOA Sophistication

*I*f you've been dutifully following along in this little book of ours, reading all about Web services and business processes and composite applications, you may have already noticed that (so far) we do a pretty good job of hiding the gnarly bits of intricate technology that make all this possible. We think, however, that you may still need to know the critical components that make SOA SOA, so we carry on.

Welcome to the SOA Registry

It may have occurred to you that somebody or something must have to keep track of all the available pieces — you know, all those services that have been garnered from your old business applications? All those reusable components have to reside somewhere, and that somewhere is the *SOA registry*.

The SOA registry is a kind of electronic catalog. It has two roles — one with respect to the operational environment and one with respect to programmers and business analysts.

In the operational environment, the SOA registry provides reference information about software components that are running or available for use. Such information is particularly important to the service broker. For programmers and business analysts, the registry acts as a reference that helps them select components and connect them together to create composite applications and build processes. Some SOA implementers grow their own registry — that is, they create their own software to provide this capability. Others purchase registry software from outside vendors.

In any case, the SOA registry also stores information about *how* each component connects to another — in other words, it documents the rules and descriptions associated with every given component.

The SOA registry is extremely important because it acts as the central reference point within a service-oriented architecture. The SOA registry contains information about all the components that the SOA supports. For that reason, it defines the "domain" of the architecture.

The SOA registry isn't just a place where you store definitions of your software components for use by your developers and business analysts. The SOA registry is where you *publish* components for more "public" entities, potentially your customers and business partners, to use.

The idea of publishing Web services is critical to SOA. You can reuse only services that are available for reuse.

Connected intimately to the registry is the SOA repository. While the registry is the central reference for all the software components within the SOA environment, the SOA repository is the central reference for all the program source code and designs that were created to build those software components. It is the ultimate reference as to what any software component does. For that reason the SOA repository becomes the hub of SOA software development activity, whether it's carried out with BPM tools or traditional programming tools.

The SOA registry and repository are so important that our *Service-Oriented Architecture For Dummies* big book gives them several chapters of their own.

Catching the Enterprise Service Bus

In service-oriented architectures, all the different pieces of software have to talk to each other. They send each other messages — and the number of messages needed for a SOA is humongous. The messages are critical to delivering end-to-end service. They must to be delivered quickly, and their arrival has to be guaranteed. If that doesn't happen, then the end-to-end service quickly becomes a lack of service.

To transport the messages between software components, SOAs often use an Enterprise Service Bus (ESB). The ESB is so important to SOA that some people think that you can't have a SOA without one, and still others think that if you have an ESB, you have a SOA. Neither statement is accurate. You don't have to have an ESB to have a SOA, but you do have to have something that plays the ESB role as far as managing messages is concerned. There are message brokers and varieties of "message-oriented middleware" that can fill this role. And an ESB does not a SOA make. If it did, we would have told you in Chapter 1. The ESB is darn important, but we barely have space to introduce it here. We dive deep into the topic in the *Service-Oriented Architecture For Dummies* big book.

The ESB is a bit like a phone system. You can think of it as a special layer that runs on top of the network, which provides a guaranteed messaging service for the most important messages on the network, including the messages that the components of SOA continuously send to each other.

Typically, in architecture diagrams, the ESB is represented as though it were a separate pipe through which information and instructions flow. (See Figure 4-1 to see what we mean.) In reality, it is not. It is a collection of software components that manage messaging from one part of the network to another. When any component wants to use the ESB, it connects to it and passes it a message in the right format, providing the address of the component to send the message to. The ESB does the rest.

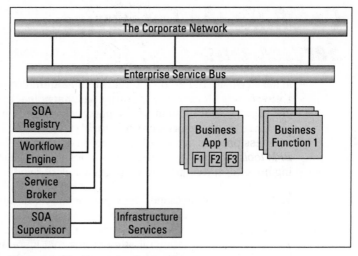

Figure 4-1: The Enterprise Service Bus.

Managing Business Process under SOA

With all this discussion of registries and buses, we want to remind you that the whole point of SOA is to make a business more manageable, more flexible and more able to change. SOA enables business people to change business processes without having to focus on the underlying technological plumbing. You can concentrate on designing and improving business processes by threading together business services. IT can build composite applications from existing business functions, adding other functions or making changes where necessary. Together, business and IT can determine the flow of work from one person to another (or from a person to a process or from a process to a person) within the larger business process.

"But how do you do that exactly?" you may wonder. Thanks for asking. With all these business processes to manage, the somewhat obvious solution is *business process management* (BPM). All by itself, BPM has contributed significantly to the liberation of business from technology. Coupled with SOA, BPM is even more powerful. BPM is the modern approach to designing and managing business processes, and many business managers and business analysts receive BPM training.

In addition to the BPM methodologies and approaches being bandied about by sharply dressed consultants in countless corporate conference rooms, you're going to find software tools out there that have been created specifically to help automate business process management. They are called, oddly enough, *BPM tools*. BPM tools organize workflows, thread together existing business functions, and create new functions.

With SOA, you want to harvest existing business functions by taking them out of their existing application homes — applications that have provided the "connective tissue" necessary to keep them functioning smoothly. The new connective tissue you need to house the harvested business functions comes in the form either of the business process itself or of a composite application. BPM tools are critical here because they help you design and manage just such business processes.

Business processes actually codify how a business works, and this very codification of business processes is a critical step for any organization subject to any kind of regulatory compliance, such as the Sarbanes-Oxley Act, the Health Insurance Portability and Accountability Act (HIPAA), and a host of others.

From the Orient

What we call BPM today is the result of a western adaptation of management best practices that evolved primarily from Japanese manufacturing. The closest equivalent Japanese term is *Kaizen*, which can be defined as "continuous improvement," or perhaps more aptly, "to take apart and put back together in a better way." Beyond continuous improvement, BPM embraces other management methods, such as Total Quality Management and Six Sigma.

BPM enables business to monitor business processes, which can lead to continuous improvement by identifying possible changes in a process that could result in better efficiency. Over time, more and more business processes are tied to software. When supported by SOA, continuous business improvement becomes a lot easier because the underlying software components are "loosely coupled," meaning that they can be changed more easily when required. When business needs to change in order to address strategic opportunities and threats, the flexible service-oriented architecture facilitates the change.

BPM tools

Different vendors orchestrate the various aspects of business process management somewhat differently, but the basic functionality has to exist for SOA to work. Here's how a BPM tool uses the components of process management to make SOA sing.

The BPM tool does three things:

- ✔ **It creates new business functions.** It may add whole new business functions or may simply add logic to run before or after an existing business function. In order to do this, the BPM tool includes some way of specifying a software process. When a new business function is created, the BPM tool adds the function's details to the SOA registry, including information about how it links to other components.

- ✔ **It links together business functions from existing applications.** The BPM tool refers to the SOA registry to identify business functions that are published there. It links them together to make composite applications or slots them in at the appropriate point in the overall workflow. The BPM tool stores this information in the SOA registry.

- ✔ **It programs the workflow engine to carry out the business process.** Using the BPM tool, business analysts design process flows and specify the movement of work from one person to another within a business process, linking in the applications that they need to use for the tasks that they have to carry out.

Figure 4-2 gives you a nice graphical representation of how a BPM tool accomplishes these three tasks.

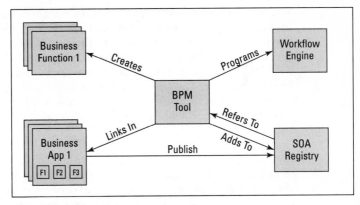

Figure 4-2: A BPM tool.

Introducing the workflow engine

The workflow engine is a software component designed to connect a whole business process from end to end, flowing work from one individual or process to another until the entire business process is carried out. Workflow development products provide a modeling capability that allows you to model a business process to produce a *workflow pattern*. The workflow pattern is, in effect, the set of instructions that the workflow engine runs.

Every business has workflow, be it casual or formal. Formalizing the workflow goes a long way to codifying business process — which is a good thing, in case you were curious. If you use BPM, you can monitor and improve the process.

Who's your service broker?

Your components are registered in the SOA registry. The workflow engine strings processes together to make things happen. What more could you need? You need a *service broker*. You have probably come across some sort of broker in your life — a real estate broker, a mortgage broker, a stock broker. The broker is the dealmaker, and the service broker brokers the deals between components. It listens very carefully to all the constraints and concerns on both sides of the equation and makes everyone happy.

The service broker is the component that actually makes all the connections between components work. It acts like a needle threading one component to the next in a business process. It uses information about the components it finds in the SOA registry and threads the components together for the workflow engine. The service broker gets things started. After it does its job of threading all the components of one business process together, it wanders off looking for another one to start.

Now we can take another look at that thing we simply referred to as the "process manager" back in Chapter 3 and see how the SOA registry, workflow engine, and service broker connect all the pieces in our new world order. (See Figure 4-3.)

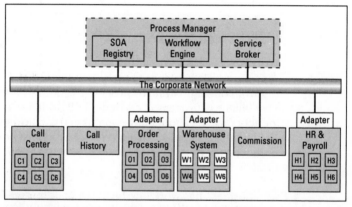

Figure 4-3: Managing the flow of a business process.

You Want Guaranteed Service?

Now that you've been exposed to some of the critical components of a service-oriented architecture, we think it's a good time to dredge up our definition of a service-oriented architecture from Chapter 2 — hopeful that it now makes more sense than it did a few chapters ago. Doing so will give focus to the vital last phrase of the definition that we have so skillfully avoided until now.

If you read Chapter 2, you may remember that we define a
service-oriented architecture as a software *architecture* for
building applications that implement business processes or
services using a set of loosely coupled black-box components
orchestrated to deliver a well-defined level of service.

The "well-defined level of service" piece comes front and
center now. Service *levels,* as the name implies, means that
service is not so black and white. You can think about service
in a restaurant (as we did in Chapter 2). You could have great
service or lousy service or so-so service. Or it might have
started out great but when it came to getting your check, your
waiter couldn't be found.

Service levels in IT have become critically important in the
last decade because business has become more and more
dependent on IT. Furthermore, IT itself has transitioned from
using autonomous software packages serving a well-defined,
limited set of users, to using software delivered as a service
over a network to huge numbers of users (just like telephone
service and electricity). And just as you know if you've ever
been caught in a power outage or experienced downed telephone lines, lack of IT service, depending on when it happens
and how long it lasts, ranges from somewhat inconvenient to
ruinous. For many organizations, an hour of IT downtime
costs millions of dollars.

Thus, businesses that depend on services often enter into
agreements with their service providers that guarantee a
specific level of service, focused primarily on the availability
and speed of service. For example, 100% uptime means that
systems are available 100% of the time (absolutely no down
time — virtually impossible).

The ability to guarantee high levels of availability and high
speeds of service usually implies higher levels of investment
in computer systems — including having redundant systems
in place in case of an emergency as well as having extra capac-
ity should the need arise. The higher the level of service, the
more it costs. So guaranteeing service availability at the
99.9999% level is significantly more costly than guaranteeing
availability at a 99% level.

And perhaps you have gleaned, being the astute reader that you are, that a *service*-oriented architecture, being, as it were, all about service, has the potential to deliver variable levels of service. Will your SOA deliver good service, bad service, so-so service, intermittent service, or unpredictable service? Obviously, anything less than good service (or maybe even great service) will put your entire business at risk.

Service-oriented architectures must make composite applications and business processes available, reliable, and predictable. Although the responsibility of all the choreography needed to make and keep service levels high falls squarely on IT, we think everybody should know the basic principles. And understanding the basic principles can go a long way toward bettering the communication flow between business and IT, which are jointly responsible in the new world order.

Application failures — Let us count the ways

Understanding service levels as they apply to application availability means understanding how and why applications fail and the consequences of the failure.

Applications can fail because the hardware they are running on fails, or the network connecting the users to the application fails. Or the application itself can fail, or the operating system running the application could fail, or some of the management software managing the application could fail.

When software components fail, it takes time to find the cause of the failure and to get the system back into action. If this can be done automatically, so much the better, but even if it can, it could take more than a minute or two. If it's not automatic, it's likely to take hours.

Not all problems cause outright failure. Some may simply slow the application down. Just as applications can fail for many reasons, they can also slow down for many reasons.

Measuring service levels

The only way to know that an application is delivering the service that the business users require is to define the service level the business needs and to measure the application's activity to see whether it is achieving it. Because application interruptions are sporadic, you need to measure service constantly and average it out over a period of a month (and/or a year) to arrive at a meaningful number.

A detailed definition of a service level for an order-processing application might be as follows:

✔ Application to be available 99.9% of the time every weekday from 6:00 a.m. to 10:00 p.m.

✔ In the event of a failure, the application should recover within 20 minutes.

✔ The response time for order inquiries, changes to orders, and entering new orders should average 1 second and should never be worse than 2 seconds, 99.9% of the time.

✔ In the event of degraded service occurring and response times slowing, normal service should be restored within 1 hour.

Defining the service level this way serves both business and IT well. Compliance with this service level agreement would mean that the order-processing application would be unavailable for, at worst, 4 hours 10 minutes during the whole year — little more than half a day. The response time could be poor for as much as 4 hours 10 minutes in the year. In the worst-case scenario, the application is unavailable for 20 minutes when it does fail. And when service degrades, it is always back to normal within an hour.

IT needs the right set of computer equipment and supporting software to deliver a service level of this kind for the application, including the appropriate failover capability as necessary. And if the application gets more users, IT needs to upgrade the computers to keep pace with the resource requirements.

End-to-end service

Delivering high levels of service for a stand-alone application isn't so tough — you have relatively few people to make happy. However, when you involve a network and begin to deliver services across that network, life ceases to be simple.

With SOA, you might (and probably will) link together components from different applications. But the service level that you want to deliver in the new application you create this way is not necessarily the same service level delivered by each of the different applications you're taking components from. In fact, they could differ from each other, and your new application could have a service level different from any of its components.

Do you have a headache yet? Consider the development of a new order-processing application that is very similar to the old one but that is written specifically to work on the Internet. You build a few new software components and use most of the components from your old order-processing system. The service levels for the old system might be acceptable, except for one thing: Because this is an Internet application, it needs to run 24/7.

So why not just leave the old application running all the time? Simply put, the old application was not built to run all the time. It was built to allow data back-ups to occur at night and for data to be extracted from the database at night when the application wasn't running.

Of course, this isn't an unmitigated disaster. You could just change the old application in some way. However, changing the old application takes time, and it will have to change again whenever your business needs change again. The reality of most businesses is that change is the only thing that is predictable. To support continuous change, linking software components together makes much more sense than recoding applications.

When you consider linking together many software components from many applications, a bigger issue emerges. The applications that were built to deliver specific service levels linked together end-to-end must deliver end-to-end service. To deliver dependable service levels means controlling the end-to-end process, which means you need the SOA supervisor.

The SOA Supervisor, again

Way back when you could barely spell SOA, we put a black box in a picture and called it the SOA supervisor. By now, you probably understand that there's a ton to control, so this SOA supervisor thingy better be good stuff. The SOA supervisor is the master conductor, the grand choreographer, the traffic cop and all-round central point of control responsible for all SOA orchestration.

Just to get a sense of who's talking to whom, think about business function components passing data and instructions to each other. At the same time, the workflow engine is passing instructions and data around. The SOA supervisor's agents are sending information to the SOA supervisor, which in turn may be communicating with plumbing services. There's a whole lot of talking going on.

Figure 4-4 shows various SOA components we talk about in this chapter. You don't need to know much about the plumbing services except that they are responsible for dealing directly with computer resources. If any of the components in the end-to-end service have any performance problems, the SOA supervisor sends the details to the plumbing services, and the plumbing services try to fix the problem. Aren't you glad that plumbing is invisible to the business?

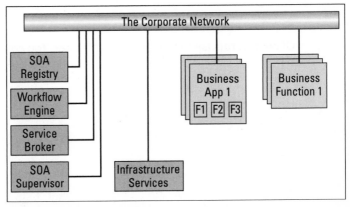

Figure 4-4: The SOA controller.

The SOA Supervisor is many things, but it is above all responsible for ensuring service levels. It uses reports from monitoring agents (initiated by the service broker) to keep track of exactly what's happening. The monitoring agents report on the service level being achieved at each point in the process. The SOA Supervisor is then in a position to know when the service degrades or when any part of it fails.

All Aboard

We think you have enough of a taste for the basics of SOA to stick your toes ever so carefully into the SOA waters. In the next two chapters, we tell you first about a real company and their SOA initiative and then tell you how you can get started. We're happy to tell you more — just look for *Service-Oriented Architecture For Dummies* (the full-sized book published by Wiley) at your favorite book retailer. We wish you every success.

Chapter 5

Real Life with SOA: Delaware Electric's True Story

● ●

In This Chapter

▶ The set-up: Working to deliver power at a lower cost

▶ Making IT the driver for business change

▶ Partnering is a good thing

▶ Keeping the customer satisfied

● ●

*W*e think the best way to get a feel for what SOA can offer is to tell you about a real-live company — one that has actually started its SOA journey. We chose a mid-sized company with revenues of $110 million and an IT staff of four. A couple of reasons we think it's a good example is that the company found that the mandate for SOA was clear and the size of the company is significant without being overwhelming. (If you want more and different examples of companies tackling SOA, we highly recommend our full-length edition of *Service-Oriented Architecture For Dummies.*)

Delaware Electric is an electric cooperative that serves 75,000 customers. Its entire staff of 140 employees includes an IT staff of only four people. Of the more than 900 electric cooperatives in the United States, Delaware Electric is one of the fastest growing — great news, of course, but its success hasn't always been easy. . . .

Big Problem # 1 occurred when the utility was deregulated. At that time, the government put a freeze on electric rates for five years, meaning that the cost of a kilowatt-hour was fixed — Delaware Electric couldn't raise the price. Now, electricity is a commodity like any other, and an electric cooperative's success depends upon delivering that commodity in a fashion that impresses its customers. Energy costs, on the other hand, are rising steadily, which means that Delaware Electric had to find ways to cut its own costs without compromising on service.

The onus of Delaware Electric's business predicament (and financial success) fell on everyone, including its Chief Financial Officer, Gary Cripps. Although responsible for Delaware Electric's small IT organization, Gary was first and foremost a businessman who viewed his *primary* responsibility as "keeping the lights on" — not only metaphorically, as in keeping Delaware Electric solvent, but literally for all 75,000 Delaware Electric customers.

Looking to IT to Solve Business Problems

Looking for ways to optimize, economize, and deliver better service, Gary closely examined the various IT systems already in use at Delaware Electric. He found lots of critical systems that didn't talk to each other. He looked around for some sort of packaged software that would simply solve the problems but found that none existed. "We simply couldn't find a software package that would handle the diversity of requirements that would provide integration for all of our business needs and would provide real-time services," is how he put it.

In addition, Gary wanted each department to be able to use the software that best fit that department's business goals — based on the best software available — and he understood that all these individual systems needed to be brought together if Delaware Electric was going to achieve the efficiencies required for a viable business.

With the help of IBM Global Services, Delaware Electric decided that SOA would help break down the barriers between various systems, allow them to leverage the critical assets they already had and provide a framework for future requirements.

As Gary said, "The primary objective was to integrate our processes across the enterprise in order to become more member-centric."

That ended up being no small feat. Delaware Electric had many packaged applications that were critical to the running of the utility. While each of these applications performed a valuable function, each was isolated from the next. Therefore, for example, they had no way to connect information about a service outage with information about which customers were impacted. They had an interactive voice response system, but it could not communicate with the system that tracked outages.

When applications can't talk to each other, people have to fill the gaps. Employees created manual processes to move between the various business functions separated by the individual applications. Faced with the necessity of cutting cost, these complex processes were a luxury Delaware Electric could no longer afford. Ironically, even if Delaware Electric had funds to add people to solve the gaps in business process, manual processes are inefficient and prone to error and would likely have had a negative impact on customer service.

Gary's team realized that they needed infrastructure software focused on integrating business processes across these isolated applications. Specifically, they wanted to integrate business processes within that part of the company responsible for everything that happens "in the field," that is, on customers' premises. For example, they wanted to be able to compare their customer information system — including the ability to load mapping data from a Geographic Information System (GIS) — with information coming from the State of Delaware. Delaware Electric needed to be able to compare this information in real time — especially when there were serious outages that could impact a huge number of consumers.

No Need to Go It Alone

The management at Delaware Electric understood that they didn't have the expertise or the staff to undertake this plan. Instead, they worked with IBM Global Services to develop a strategic plan. Delaware Electric's management worked with three folks from IBM — one project manager and two developers. Working together, the team developed a customer-focused plan that identified key business processes. They then mapped the process plan to the various applications across the organization.

To manage power outages, they had to link the customer database and the field engineering database, and they needed a way to connect both of these applications with the company's interactive voice response system. All of these systems had to be integrated with all of the processes throughout the company. Delaware Electric's management understood that they could benefit greatly from changing the focus of their IT systems to support efficient customer service, but that meant shifting the focus away from the billing system that had been the primary focus.

The experts at IBM recommended using an IBM WebSphere Enterprise Service Bus (ESB) as a way to link packaged applications to each other. In this first phase, Delaware Electric used Web service interfaces to hook its various packaged applications into the service bus. This required both the subject matter experts within Delaware Electric and the IBM consultants working with the package software vendors to connect these applications into the service bus. As a result, Delaware Electric's PR department can say, "We can now provide more services to our customers."

The Journey Continues

At the time of this writing, Delaware Electric has completed Phase One of its journey. Its employees have integrated the outage management system with the geographic information system and the field management system. In the next phase, they will integrate the customer information systems into the WebSphere Enterprise Service Bus. Within the next 18 months, they will install automated meter-reading equipment and connect it into the enterprise service.

Reflecting on how Delaware Electric's SOA plan will benefit its customers, Gary says this:

> Imagine that you are an individual who is in the
> process of adding an addition to your home. You
> need the electric company to tell your contractor
> where the electric hookup is on your property
> and you need them to come out and work with
> the contractor to plan for the extension of power
> to the addition. With the new process and the
> enterprise service bus in place, you will be able
> to call Delaware Electric and have the clerk at the
> call center go into the application, look up your
> house, view where the hookup is and tell you
> when the technician is scheduled to arrive. The
> call center clerk will not have to know how each
> of these systems works; he or she will simply be
> able to fluidly move from one function to another.
> The customer gets the information they need in a
> timely manner and everyone is happy.

With the focus on customer service, the folks at Delaware
Electric believe that SOA will help their customers minimize
energy costs. With the new SOA environment, customers will
be able to go to the Web and view their own energy consump-
tion. They will be able to see when peak energy times occur
and schedule major energy use (such as a printing production
run) for a time where energy usage is low and thereby save
money. Gary continues:

> If a consumer has an electrical problem, I want
> my call center representative to be able to deter-
> mine whether there is a problem with our system
> or a problem within the customer's home. If we
> have to dispatch a high-priced lineman only to
> discover that the problem is unrelated, everyone
> loses. On the other hand, if the call center repre-
> sentative can inform the customer that they
> should call their own electrician rather than wait-
> ing for hours to be told that "it's not my prob-
> lem," the utility saves money by not sending out
> the expensive union employee and the consumer
> has the right person fixing the right problem at
> the right time.

Now, that's progress!

Summing Up

Delaware Electric's business problems were ripe for SOA — but it took an astute management to recognize the need and opportunity. The acute problem of needing to cut costs while at the same time delivering better service led them to take a close look at their entire company. Understanding that a great deal of their problems stemmed from the fact that the applications in the various parts of the company "couldn't talk to each other" — and that if they could, the whole company would benefit — was key to selecting SOA. In some ways, Delaware Electric was lucky — they recognized the value and knew they didn't have the resources to tackle it on their own. Buy-in from senior management is critical to SOA success.

Chapter 6

SOA Quick Start: Entry Points for Starting the SOA Journey

*I*f you're eager to start your SOA journey, we have two strong caveats about what you *shouldn't* do:

> ✔ **Don't try to boil the ocean.** That is, don't attempt to do everything at once.

> ✔ **Don't turn SOA over to the IT organization and wash your hands of it.** For SOA to be effective, it must be done from the top down. In other words, if you really want your SOA plan to succeed, business management and IT must work together.

So, how should you approach SOA? You need a SOA plan that combines a business perspective, a technology road-map, and an organizational initiative. Rather than give you a philosophical discussion, we give you some practical guide-lines for getting started with SOA.

Map Your Organization's Business Structure

One of the biggest differences between planning for SOA and planning for any other technology initiative is that SOA planning forces you to think differently about your own company, your industry, your ability to innovate, and the value of technology.

What is your company anyway? Are you in the retail business? If so, do you manufacture the products you sell, or do you sell products from a variety of manufacturers? Are you a financial services company? If so, do you put forth one type of offering? Do you have a strong set of partners that you collaborate with? Are you a distribution company? If so, what makes you different from other companies in your market? And what does it actu-ally mean to be "different" in your market? Finally, how should an innovative company act tomorrow and in ten years?

Start your journey by stepping back and figuring out what your company is really about. How does this translate into the core business services that define your business? Most businesses have key factors that have made them successful over time. SOA structure requires you to think from the concept of reuse. In order to think from reuse, you need to capture the way the business can be structured as a set of services. Think about how to define your own business as a set of discrete services.

The good news is that you probably don't have to start from scratch. Many vendors have done a lot of work to create maps particular to specific kinds of companies and are happy to help you get started. (You probably don't want to try to tackle SOA without *some* help.)

Chances are your SOA vendor can help you get started with a map for companies like yours. Compare one of these maps to your own company and then modify the particulars that make your company different from the model. Voilà — you now have a view of your company as a set of business services. This map helps you figure out where to start. When developing a map specific to your company, include the following steps:

> ✔ Discover and gather business requirements.
>
> ✔ Simulate and optimize the business process of your company.
>
> ✔ Determine what you need to measure in order to determine how well your business is performing.

We know these steps sound simultaneously simplistic and grandiose. We apologize. It's the nature of the beast. SOA is chock-full of simple ideas that alter the world. They represent a whole new way of doing IT-enabled business. They represent a new world order, and that new world order requires thinking in a new way for many organizations.

Pick Your Initial SOA Targets to Gain Experience and Demonstrate Success

If you try to move your entire company to SOA overnight, you'll likely end up living your own worst nightmare. Instead, start by reviewing the business services map to identify your first target. Select a specific area where you can leverage existing software assets, turn them into services, and create a plan that demonstrates the value of the flexibility that you will gain from SOA. You don't need to start with something huge. Remember, you're proving that SOA works in your organization and that it has real value.

For example, we know an insurance company that chose its Claims Processing department as its first SOA implementation. It turned its claims processing process into a business service called *claims processing*. By making it easy to change provider information, the company was able to add new claims providers in a few weeks rather than the 24 months it had taken previously. This allowed the company to add new partners quickly and to expand revenue. In addition, the company was able to offer this flexible and rapid claims processing service to other companies, providing a new source of revenue for the company.

We recommend that you pick a high-profile area where you can see results quickly. Demonstrating the benefits of SOA can make business change much less painful. You might have many good choices about where to start. One company might need to create a portal or a specialized Web site that brings key business services together to meet an immediate business objective. The portal view can help create an entirely different user experience within an organization. Another company may need to provide a single view of customer data so that various departments, subsidiaries, and business partners can find creative ways to grow revenue by focusing on customer opportunities to up sell and cross sell. Other companies may choose to focus on getting the necessary architectural components in place to support their movement to SOA. Still others may look at the manageability of process and security or corporate governance.

We could list hundreds of different options — all of them perfectly appropriate for a particular company or concern — but you, and you alone, know best what will have the greatest impact for your organization. Figure out what will get the biggest bang for your buck and go for it.

Prepare Your Organization for SOA

No matter where you start, all roads lead to the people. SOA is about how people across organizations work together to change the way they think about the intersection of business and technology. In this regard, the organizational issues are much more important than any single technology issue. Often, departments within organizations work in isolation, and corporate structures have been designed to emphasize departmental objectives rather than cross-departmental cooperation. For SOA to succeed, organizations need a new way to think about the value of technology, one driven by a corporate-wide effort to approach technology differently.

In order to kickstart such a new approach, we recommend establishing working groups that span departments. Separating work by different parts of the organization doesn't work. Information cannot be owned by one department — it is a corporate asset; likewise with business services. Business services must be valuable across many different departments. We recommend that top management establish SOA as a corporate mandate and set up an organizational structure and recognition program that rewards cooperation. If your company isn't at that stage, find high-profile departmental executives who can set an example. You'll need to approach different areas from different points of view.

IT Developers Need to Learn a Different Approach

Most IT developers are used to writing code that lives within its own enclosed world. When an organization begins the movement to SOA, developers need to start writing software based on the assumption that it will be used in many different circumstances. This is not necessarily an intuitive approach for developers who come from the old school of doing things. Part of preparing the development organization is helping them understand how the business might use the components they will be asked to build. Developers should be teamed with business professionals across the organization to help them change to a more global perspective.

Business Managers Need to Look beyond Their Own Departments

Business managers tend to worry about their own department's goals and objectives and the metrics that they are judged on. SOA involves thinking creatively about business process and business measurements. In order to appropriately identify key business processes, you need strong cooperation and collaboration between departments and divisions.

Business Partners Are Part of the SOA Success Story

In a highly competitive business world, no company is safe without partners. SOA can play an important part in making partnerships innovative. Any company that has a SOA strategy needs to implement the strategic plan in conjunction with its business partners. Partners need to be educated on the value of the strategy and how it will help them take advantage of the combined strengths that partnerships can create.

Don't Enter SOA Alone

We have tried to emphasize that SOA is a journey, not a one-time project to be implemented by a single department to get a quick hit or quick success. It is a corporate-wide process to leverage technology in a way that reflects the business's key business processes, enabling business to change when needed without being constrained by technology. Therefore, don't approach SOA in isolation. We recommend that you find yourself some help Look for technology suppliers that have created successful SOA implementations for companies like yours. You probably won't be able to find a single vendor that can provide you with everything you need. Look for companies that can create an easy-to-implement package and that are based on standards so that you can add and subtract pieces as your implementation matures.

Look for models of SOA success. What can you glean from companies that have already started on their SOA journeys? What would they do differently? What has worked well for them? How have they managed to get their people to work together toward a common goal?

Off to the Races

We hope we've given you enough to whet your appetite for SOA. We go a long way toward fleshing out what's here in our full-length edition of *Service-Oriented Architecture For Dummies,* so if we've left you wanting to know more, you'll know just where to look.

We believe that a service-oriented architecture will be critical for any business today that relies on technology to run the business. The world is changing rapidly and SOA helps an organization keep pace. It's SOA that can help "future-proof" a company — make it ready and able to change when change inevitably comes.

We hope this little book has been helpful to you and we hope you take a look at our big book. Until then, SOA long . . .